FAMOUS
WOMEN

OF

NORTH
STAFFORDSHIRE

by

Patricia Pilling

INTRODUCTION

This book is written in honour of those women who have done so much to contribute, not only to the history of Stoke-on-Trent, but also to the corporate identity of womanhood and their ability to achieve. Whether that achievement is small or great it is still to be celebrated. I hope this book is an encouragement to you. Where others have achieved, you can too.

It is dedicated with loving care to both my parents, Margaret and Arthur Pilling, whose lifelong encouragement of me has contributed so much to the person I am today. Although they have now passed from this earth, my mother at Christmas and my father at Easter, their love is always with me and mine with them. This book is for them.

My thanks go also particularly to Mary, my sister, for her support but also to the rest of my family and all my friends and colleagues who have believed in me! Thanks to John Abberley for his advice, to Anthea Turner for her time and personal interest in my work. Thanks to all those who allowed me to interview them and to all the people recorded in this book for showing how much the women of North Staffordshire can achieve!

© Patricia Pilling 1999
ISBN 1 897949 55 3

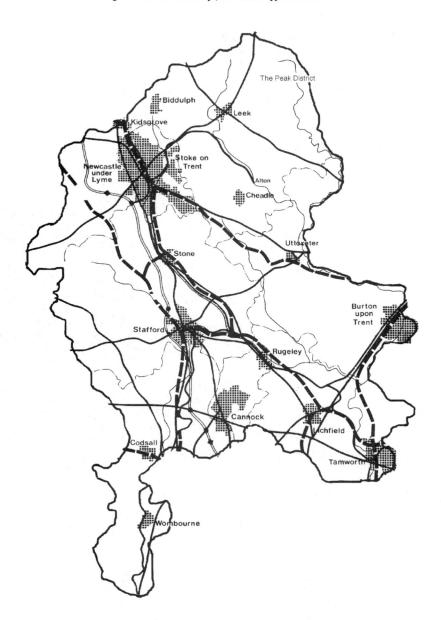

A simple map of Staffordshire showing the modern day conurbations. North Staffordshire is famous for its pottery industry and for the Staffordshire Moorlands at the southerly tip of the Pennine chain.

CONTENTS

THE BIZARRE GIRLS
1930s

MILLICENT
SUTHERLAND'S
AMBULANCE PARTY AT
NAMUR IN OCCUPIED
BELGIUM
1914

THE NICE
GIRLS
1993

ANGLO-SAXON STAFFORDSHIRE

CHESHIRE

DERBYSHIRE

Longnor

Newtown

Hartington

Leek

Steeplow

Welton

Throwley
Hall

Calton

Audley

Wetley

The

Ramshorn

Betley

Potteries

Newcastle
under Lyme

Cheadle

Madeley

Longton

Forsbrook

Alton

Hanford

Bradley

Barlaston

Fulford

Mucklestone

Stone

Hilderstone

Uttoxeter

Standon

Milwich

Marchington

Dove

High Offley

Newborough

Stretton

Stafford

Burton upon Trent

Norbury

Sow

Talenhill

Branston

Stapenhill

Coppenhall

Walton

Penkridge

Longdon

Wychnor

Cannock

Chase

Elford

Lichfield

Shareshill

SHROPSHIRE

Tamworth

Wolverhampton

Walsall

Tipton

West
Bromwich

Himley

Dudley

WARWICKSHIRE

WORCESTERSHIRE

CHAPTER ONE

ST WERBURGH

In Anglo-Saxon times the Midland region, then known as Mercia, was ruled by King Wulfhere from 659-675 AD. Wulfhere, who lived in a palace at Bury Bank just outside of Stone, had two sons, Wolfad and Ruffian, and one daughter, Werburgh, the Princess of Mercia. Although living much of her early life at Bury Bank she is said to have been born at Trentham (Tricingham) which later was the site of one of the monasteries she founded.

Mercia was established by Penda the Great, grandfather to Werburgh when the Romans withdrew from Britain and the Saxons invaded and drove out the Celtic Briton inhabitants. Mercia, under Penda the Great's rule, became the dominant kingdom in England in the 7th Century.

Penda the Great was succeeded by his eldest son Penda following his father's death in a battle with the King of Northumbria. Penda was a pagan who worshiped the gods Woden and Thor, but he married a Christian, the daughter of the King of York, and was converted.

Penda was succeeded by Peda who was also a Christian. Peda was murdered and was the succeeded by Wulfhere, Penda's son. The Kingdom of Mercia, although for a long time pagan, was gradually becoming Christian, and Werburgh herself was very influenced by her mother's faith.

Werburgh's two brothers, Wulfad and Ruffian, became converted to Christianity as young men. The story is related of how whilst hunting in Needwood Forest the two brothers became lost and night-bound and were found by Chad, the famous missionary who is reputed to have brought Christianity to England. Chad offered them hospitality and during their stay shared with them the gospel of Christ. Both brothers became Christians and when they returned to their father, told him their good news. Wulfhere was very angry, so angry in fact that he had both his sons killed. The two princes were buried, according to Saxon custom, under a pile of stones in the small town of Staines, now Stone. In later years a priory was built on the site and in 1251 it was granted a market charter to hold a weekly market. It remained the centre of the town until the dissolution of the Priory in 1537.

Wulfhere later regretted his murderous actions and became a Christian himself in his remorse, following which the whole of the Midlands region

A tapestry of St Werburgh recalling the legend of how the saint restored to life one of her geese, stolen and killed by a servant.

was opened up to the gospel. Princess Werburgh decided to give her whole life to Christ.

After Wulfhere's death his successor Aethelred became King. Aethelred was Wulfhere's much younger brother and Werburgh's uncle, but they had been reared as brother and sister. He charged Werburgh with the task of continuing to convert Mercia to Christianity and in due course when he became King of England, the rest of the country. Werburgh first spent several years in preparation for her life's mission, through prayer and meditation in a monastery in the Fens, before moving to Repton the capital of Mercia where her ministry really began.

Werburgh founded monasteries at Repton, Weedon, Trentham, Crowland and Hanbury, and she refounded the monastery in Peterburgh. Her favourite was always Hanbury, near Burton on Trent, built in AD 680.

Werburgh spent her life spreading Christianity and doing good works. Many miracles are accorded to her, famous amongst them being when she prayed for the restoration to life of one of a favourite gaggle of geese which had been stolen and killed by a servant. Its 're-birth' is recorded on tapestries and pictures in several sacred sites including the Cathedral at Chester. The symbol of St Werburgh is a flock of geese.

Werburgh was probably the first nun in this area. She set an example of holiness and goodness to be followed by other single Christian women who chose to use their lives for God, and as a result much of the religious life at that time became dominated by women.

For their living, she and her community at Hanbury mined salt, bred animals for sale and sheep for wool, and mined gypsum which was sent abroad for sale.

Werburgh died in AD 699 of natural causes at 50 years of age. She died at the monastery at Trentham where her body was preserved and where they wished to keep her with them because of their love of her, and also as they knew it would bring them great acclaim in the future. However, she had written in her will that she wished to be buried at Hanbury and whilst Trentham slept, the body of Werburgh was stolen and taken back home.

In 708 a splendid shrine was built at Hanbury commemorating her life, and great wealth came to Hanbury as gifts were given to the shrine. Effigies and statues of St Werburgh can still be seen there. Werburgh lay at Hanbury undisturbed for many years until the Viking invasions. The nuns and monks heard of how the monasteries on the East Coast had been destroyed and so they feared for the body of Werburgh, and that her grave and remains would be desecrated. It was decided, because Hanbury could not be defended, that Werburgh should be moved to somewhere fortified where her body could be protected. Chester was chosen.

When they dug up Werburgh's body it was discovered that her remains were still intact and preserved, and this was seen as another miracle. The journey from Hanbury to Chester lasted 5 days and churches were prepared in her name to receive the body and retinue on each of the nights during the journey. The first stop was the monastery at Trentham and then at Kingsley where the church still bears her name.

On arrival in Chester, Werburgh was laid in a church later the site of the monastery founded by the Norman invaders, the Abbey of St. Werburgh, and

now known as Chester Cathedral. A chapel to her name remains there to this day. But St Werburgh's history is rooted very much in the area of Stoke-on-Trent and Stone. There are many testimonies to her in the naming of churches, schools and roads throughout the area. She was one of the most famous persons of her day and we in North Staffordshire owe an important part of our heritage to this lady who gave up her life as a Princess, for a life of work and goodness following Christ.

The shrine of St Werburgh in the Lady Chapel at Chester Cathedral. It has been a site for Christian pilgrimage for centuries and remains so today.

CHAPTER TWO

MRS CRAIK

During the Victorian era, Mrs Craik, born Dinah Mullock, was one of the most successful and prominent writers of novels. She produced no less than thirty novels, the most famous of which was "John Halifax, Gentleman". She also wrote nine books of short stories, three anthologies of poetry and nine collections of 'Thoughts and Observations'. As a result of her prolific writing career, Mrs Craik achieved a measure of financial success and independence that would be the envy of any modern day authoress and was remarkable in her day. She was greatly admired by the literary public and, in recognition of the public and royal approval of her work, she was granted a pension from the Queen.

It is said that the experience of Dinah's early life had been the creative force for her desire to succeed as a writer and to be a financially, and socially, independent woman. The family life in which she was brought up was fraught with marital tension and stress, largely due to her father's mental ill health. It was out of this experience that Dinah found the capacity, not only to endure, but also to create a meaningful life for herself. She said that she always felt 'conscious of a vocation for authorship' and certainly, once the opportunity presented itself, she pursued this vocation with verve and vigour.

Dinah's early life had not augured well for the stability and well-being of the family. She was born at Longfield Cottage, Hartshill and it was Dinah's mother who was eventually to be the mainstay of her life, providing for not only her immediate material and emotional needs, but planning ahead for both her development as a person and her ability to survive financially. Dinah's mother was Dinah Mellard. She came from a well-known Newcastle-under-Lyme family, the owners of a tannery business in Pool Dam. In 1825 she met and married Thomas Mullock, son of Robert Mullock and of Irish gentry origins. This union proved to be the undoing of Dinah Mellard although possibly the grounding for her daughter's will to achieve.

Thomas Mullock was undoubtedly a talented and intelligent man. He had been a Comptroller of the Stamp Office in Dublin before he came to England to be further educated. He matriculated from Oxford in 1817 and moved to Liverpool to pursue a business career. He became involved in

Abel Fletcher's Mill at
Tewkesbury today, made
famous by Mrs Craik's "John
Halifax, Gentleman".

The memorial to Mrs Craik in
Tewkesbury Abbey.

politics and was noticed by the MP Lord Canning who admired his gifts of speech. He became part of his secretarial staff but quickly tired of this and returned to writing pamphlets and preaching, an interest he had developed at Oxford.

Thomas's first public religious meeting was in the Potteries and it was here he met and married Dinah Mellard. Married life began quietly enough but Thomas's eccentric and extrovert personality and behaviour soon led to him being imprisoned in Stafford Gaol for libel. By 1832 his wife had had enough and turned him out of their home. He was committed to Stafford County Asylum as a pauper lunatic where he remained for seven years. The family was reconciled for a time on his release in 1840. The family then moved to London but again separated in 1845.

Mrs Mullock had learned classics for herself and taught this to others. She set up a school for girls at which her daughter assisted, and during these years Dinah discovered her love of literature and writing. Mrs Mullock was a financially astute, as well as an intelligent, woman, and had ensured that all the family property was made over to her legally. As a consequence, on her death in October 1845, Dinah was left a small legacy providing a certain basis for her survival, upon which Dinah set out to build her future career as a writer.

Her first novel, 'The Ogilvies' was published anonymously in 1849 and was an instant success. Others followed: 'Olive' (1850), 'The Head of the Family' (1851), 'Alice Learmont', 'A Fairy Tale' (1852), 'Agatha's Husband' (1853) and in 1856, 'John Halifax, Gentleman', her most successful and famous novel. It was translated into French, German, Italian, Greek and Russian and was a classic in its day and is still considered so by many. Some contemporary critics judged her at times the equal of Charles Dickens - "she displayed eloquence, pathos, a subdued genial humour and a happy dilineation of character...... But for a wider observation of life and manners she would have been placed in the highest rank of novelists."

Her success was rapid. She was soon noted by Oliphant to be *'a writer with a recognised position.'* She mixed with many famous people of the day like Holman Hunt, Lord Morley and Sir Noel Parton, moving easily in fashionable literary circles and soirées. She was admired by Jane Carlyle for her self assurance and independence, phenomena which were not common amongst the female sex in the Victorian era.

In 1861 Dinah met George Lillie Craik, a son of old friends and a partner in the Macmillan Publishing Company. George at this time was involved in a railway accident which was to disable him for life. Dinah nursed him after the accident and during this time the two fell in love. They were married in 1864. Dinah now felt the emotional fulfilment she desired.

However, she still continued to pursue her career as a writer, maintaining her financial independence. Mrs Craik guarded her marriage and private life carefully and, therefore, little is known of this. She lived with her husband at the 'Corner House' in Shortlands in Kent. She and George did not have children of their own but they did adopt a baby, Dorothy, who had been left on their doorstep.

Mrs Craik died on 12th October 1887 following a heart attack, four weeks prior to Dorothy's wedding. She is buried in Keston Churchyard in Kent and there is a bas relief portrait and inscribed tablet celebrating her life and works in Tewkesbury Abbey, Tewkesbury being the setting for 'John Halifax, Gentleman'.

Dinah Mullock - Mrs Craik - achieved an enormous amount in her lifetime, in pursuit of her dreams and ambitions. She was fully of the opinion that women should be made to recognise their 'right of independence' both through education and professional opportunities. She encouraged women to pursue work that challenged them, that enabled them to be self-reliant, free agents. In 1864 she set aside a trust for women authors less fortunate than herself.

This Victorian Potteries girl had set an example for women to both admire and emulate.

Mrs Craik at a time when she was a nationally famous authoress.

CHAPTER THREE

MILLICENT, DUCHESS OF SUTHERLAND

Although Millicent, Duchess of Sutherland, was not born in Stoke-on-Trent, she was a woman who had a major impact on its history and social development which should not go unrecorded.

Born in Fife, at Dysart House on 20th October 1867, Millicent was the daughter of the 4th Earl of Rosslyn and Blanche Fitzroy who was descended from Charles II. Her full name was Millicent Frances St Clair-Erskine. Millicent was only 17 when she met and married Cromartie Sutherland Leveson Gower, Marquess of Stafford and heir to the 3rd Duke of Sutherland with homes at Dunrobin Castle, Sutherland, Scotland, Trentham Hall, Lilleshall Hall, and Stafford House, The Mall, London. For those living in the Dresden area of Stoke on Trent it can be easily seen where the names of many of the streets came from.

Following their marriage in 1884, the Duke and Duchess spent their early years together at the house in Tittensor Chase. Millicent had four children during her marriage, Victoria Elizabeth (1885-8), George Granville (1888-1963) later the 5th Duke of Sutherland, Alistair St. Clair (1890-1921) and Rosemary Millicent (1893-1930).

Young Millicent quickly became famous as a society hostess, being both beautiful and diplomatic, but it is not for this that we remember her. It is rather for her social conscience and the practical way in which she tackled pain and suffering that she has made her mark in Stoke-on-Trent.

Millicent, at one time nicknamed 'Meddlesome Millie' by employers who resented her campaigns against injustice, took it upon herself to challenge the dangerous practices of many pottery industries. One of her main campaigns was against the use of lead-based glazes by pottery workers which often led to chronic poisoning. Millicent continued fighting this until the lead glazes were eventually banned earning her the further hostility of the manufacturers. Arnold Bennett, in his famous pottery novels, parodies her, albeit gently, and presents her as 'Interfering Iris, the Countess of Chell':

'The Countess at this period was busying herself with the policemen of the Five Towns. In her exhaustless passion for philanthropy, bazaars, and platforms, she had already dealt with orphans, the aged, the blind,

THE POTTERIES CRIPPLES' GUILD was established some eight years ago for the relief and assistance of Crippled Children amongst the poorer classes in the Pottery towns. To-day this Guild has the names of nearly 400 children on its books, and is divided into three divisions, all of which merit the attention and interest of the public.

Firstly, there is the Convalescent Home at Woore, where sometimes for months spinal cases, hip cases and deformities of other kinds are treated, and the children, by good food and by healthy air and happy surroundings, are restored to a large measure of activity, and indeed, save in exceptional cases, to complete health.

The nine beds in this Home are filled by boys and girls sent from various districts in North Staffordshire, not always from the Pottery towns, although preference is given when possible to children from these towns. It is hoped, if more money is forthcoming, to increase the number of beds to eleven.

Secondly, there are Voluntary Committees in the towns of Hanley, Stoke, Longton, Fenton, Burslem and Tunstall. The ladies who belong divide amongst themselves the onerous duties of visiting the Cripples in their districts; they become friends of the children, and report on their wants to the General Secretary or to the Honorary Medical Officer. Nourishing food is given at discretion, and a successful endeavour has been made to teach those crippled children who are fairly active the rudiments of needlework and other light forms of employment in Spare-Time Classes.

The ladies on these Committees are really carrying on a labour of love, and money is urgently needed by them to supply surgical instruments to the children under their charge, and to give them an oft-needed change at the seaside or in the country, for it may well be understood that the Woore Home with only nine beds cannot receive them all.

Extract from Foreword to 1908 Bazaar Programme

potter's asthma, creches, churches, chapels, schools, economic cookery, the smoke-nuisance, country holidays, Christmas puddings and blankets, healthy musical entertainments, and barmaids. The excellent and beautiful creature was suffering from a dearth of subjects when the policemen occurred to her. She made the benevolent discovery that policemen were overworked, underpaid, courteous, and trustworthy public servants, and that our lives depended on them. And from this discovery it naturally followed that policemen deserved her energetic assistance.

and again,

'Denry observed that the Countess was now a different woman. She had suddenly put on a manner to match her costume, which in certain parts was stiff with embroidery. From the informal companion and the tamer of mules she had miraculously developed into the public celebrity, the peeress of the realm, and the inaugurator-general of philanthropic schemes and buildings. Not one of the important male personages but would have looked down on Denry! And yet, while treating Denry as a jolly equal the Countess with all her embroidered and stiff politeness somehow looked down on the important male personages - and they knew it. And the most curious thing was that they seemed to rather enjoy it.'

(Arnold Bennett, 'The Card')

Putting this light humour aside, there is no doubt that Millicent had a genuine interest in the welfare of others and particularly those who were poor, sick and downtrodden. Millicent began the campaign to help, and if possible cure, the seriously crippled poor children of the district through the formation in 1901 of the Potteries and Newcastle Cripples' Guild. This later became the North Staffs Cripples' Aid Society and led to what became the North Staffordshire Orthopaedic Hospital. She was also responsible for the development of the Hanchurch Convalescent Home and Hospital for Children, which provided free holidays in the countryside for sick children, and the Cripples' Convalescent Home at Woore.

Millicent's work was later taken over by her daughter, Rosemary Ednam who, as the new president of the Cripples' Aid Society, aimed to raise £20,000 for a new Outpatients Department at the Orthopaedic Hospital. She was, however, killed in a plane crash only a few months after making her target public, but instead of the project folding the donations poured in and the department was opened in 1929 by the Prince of Wales.

During the First World War Millicent was the first of the aristocracy to establish an overseas hospital unit under the auspices of the Red Cross. She initially travelled to France but immediately transferred to work in a hospital in Belgium. Here she found a fully equipped hospital and enough nurses to cope with the present need, so she volunteered to work in the provinces. This required her to resign from the Red Cross so that she could take small ambulances of nurses into the remoter occupied districts. Millicent wired to England for a surgeon, trained nurses and funds and so began the 'Millicent Sutherland Ambulance.' She now worked under the Belgian 'Service de Sante de l'Armee'. At one point, she became caught up in the hostilities and was detained by the Germans, but was later allowed to escape from the area, helped in no small way by her ability to speak both French and German fluently. For her effort in the War Millicent received the Croix de Guerre.

Millicent was also a very literary person. She wrote her first book when she was 20, called 'How I spent my 20th year' and was a biography of her voyage around the world and the things she had seen and learned during the time. She wrote novels, biographies, poems and plays as well as newspaper and magazine articles. Her works include 'One Hour and the Next' (1899), 'On the Dangerous Processes in the Potting Industry' (in 'The Staffordshire Potter', H. Owen), 'The Winds of the World' (1902), 'Six Weeks at the War' (1914). and 'That Fool of a Woman' (1925). Millicent's most prestigious play was 'The Conqueror' (1905) which was sent under a pseudonym to the famous actor/manager Sir Johnston Forbes-Robertson who agreed to stage it at La Scala, London. Millicent only later revealed her real identity when she was contacted with regard to technical changes. The story was of a tyrant and warlord, Morven, who sought to dominate and rule the world. It was set to music by Edward German. It ran at La Scala for 12 performances. Millicent thought that she had achieved critical acclaim at last. The short run did not deter her from continuing with her literary endeavours. She continued to mix in literary circles, inviting many famous authors of the day, including J.M. Barrie, to stay with her at Trentham Hall.

Millicent was also concerned with encouraging other women in their literary talents and took part in the Womens' Journalist Society and was, for a time, the President. She opened her home, Stafford House, to the members of the Womens' Congress of 1899. Although not a self proclaimed suffragette, Millicent was concerned to ensure that barriers to equality were challenged and that women were encouraged to achieve their greatest potential.

Her direct influence in the Potteries ended in 1911 when Trentham Hall was demolished. Her influence has continued in many other ways though, and she should be remembered for her social conscience and the positive way in which she transformed her beliefs into action.

Millicent lived her later years in France, a country she had come to love, until she died in 1955 at her summer home, La Maisou, Sauverterre-de-Bern. A memorial window to her is situated in Dornach Cathedral and portraits of her can be found at Dunrobin Castle, by Ellis Roberts, and in New York, by the American painter, John Singer Sargent.

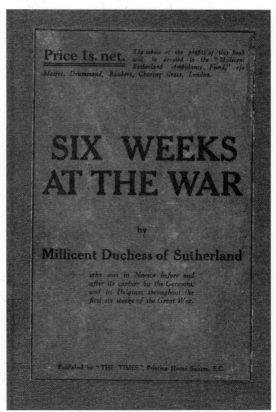

The cover of 'Six Weeks at the War'.

The cover of the official Bazaar and Fête programme for 1908 which raised many thousands of pounds for the Duchess of Sutherland's Potteries Cripples' Guild and Home for Crippled Children. The A4 size programme ran to over 200 pages.

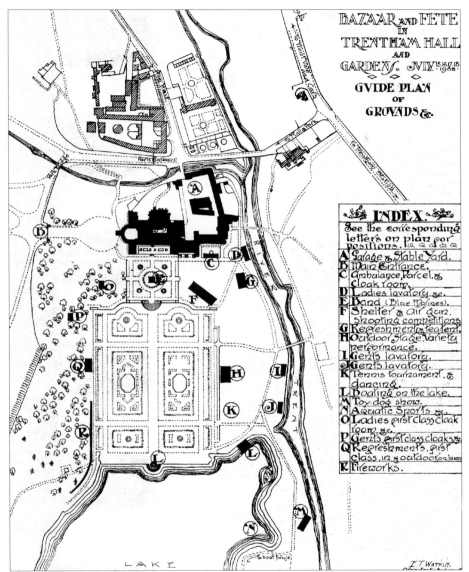

The Guide Plan from the Bazaar programme gives an impression of the scale of the Bazaar and Fête. The black silhouette middle upper page is Trentham Hall itself and there were 50 stands and refreshment points in the Hall. The event lasted for four days, the admission on the first day was 5s., 1s. on the second day and 6d. on the 3rd and 4th days. Special trains were laid on to Trentham by the North Staffordshire, LNW, Midland, Great Western and Great Northern railway companies with buses running from the station and tram terminus all day. There were literally hundreds of events including a Grand Water Carnival in the Lake, variety shows, concerts and plays in the Hall and the Park, fireworks displays, and the Bands of the Royal Marines and of the 1st Staffordshire Royal Field Artillery.

CHAPTER FOUR

GERTIE GITANA

'Gertie Gitana', born Gertrude Astbury, was by the age of 14 the sensation of the day, receiving top billing in music halls up and down the land.

Gertie was born at 7 Shirley Street, Longport, but moved when only a few months old, with her parents, to 50 Price Street, Burslem. Her mother, Lavinia, was a teacher at St. Peter's Roman Catholic school, Cobridge. Her father was a foreman in a pottery works in Hanley. It was from these humble beginnings that a star was born.

Gertie made her first stage appearance at the age of four with the Thomas Tomkinson's Royal Gipsy Children, an entertainment troupe. Here she not only sang but also danced, and impressed the audiences with her male impersonation act. It was here that she was named, "Little Gitana" which means "Little Gypsy".

Gertie soon became the star of the show. Whilst appearing in Manchester she was 'spotted' by Lily Lonsdale who had many friends in the musical world. Two of these were Belle and James O'Connor who, impressed by Gertie's talent, went immediately to her parents to persuade them to let Gertie go with them on their travelling show. The Astburys were, understandably, more than a little anxious at the thought of Gertie travelling far and wide and in the company of a couple they barely knew. Gertie was after all only about eight years of age at this time! Reluctantly Gertie's parents agreed and Gertie went off to join the O'Connors team at the Tivoli Theatre in Barrow-in-Furness.

The Grand Theatre in Hanley.

Gertie's great 'break' came at the age of ten when she was performing with the team at the Lyceum Theatre in London. One of the billed stars was unable to perform one night and Gertie was asked to take over the spot. Her trademark by this time had become performing in a white silk top hat, but it was the time of the Boer War and Gertie brought the house down with a rendition of a song depicting the return of 'Her Soldier Daddy', dressed in a soldier's uniform. The result was an enormous tug at the heart strings of the early twentieth century audience. She became a sensation overnight with her beautiful soprano voice. By the time she was fourteen she was regularly 'topping the bill' and earning what would now be a fantastic wage.

It was at this time she changed her name to 'Gertie Gitana' retaining some of her real name and some of the history that had served her so well up to this point. It was also maintaining links with her family that brought her her next two successes.

Gertie had a brother who lived in America. It was he who introduced Gertie to the saxophone, a totally new instrument invented by Mr A. Sax and which was at that time a major influence in America in the development of the Jazz Movement. Having been sent a saxophone all the way from America, Gertie began to learn to play it and eventually included it in her act. This was no mean feat for Gertie was only five feet one tall. The crowds loved it!

It was again her contact with America which brought her next success. Her brother sent her a copy of a song that had hitherto only been played in America. But it was not only its newness but its great sentimentality which caused it to be such a success with Gertie's public. The song was 'Nellie Dean', for which she, and also Gracie Fields, are so well known today. It is said that Gertie's rendition of this song and her *'ability to take an audience by storm'* was one of Gracie Field's greatest inspirations.

Gertie was, by this time, only sixteen years of age and is said to be one of the only variety artistes ever to to succeed at the Lyceum Theatre. Her repertoire also included 'Silver Bell', 'Sweet Caroline', 'When the Harvest Moon is Shining' and 'Never Mind' which were her favourite songs, but it is possibly 'Nellie Dean' for which she will always be remembered.

The First World War arrived and Gertie, later described by one of her theatrical friends as *'the kindest, gentlest little lady I think I have ever met'* immediately went to work raising thousands of pounds through the sale of

The Theatre Royal
at Hanley and
Gertie in the latter
part of her career.

her picture postcards, to pay for comforts for wounded soldiers.

Gertie's popularity continued. In 1926, despite opposition from Belle O'Connor, she starred opposite Don Ross, the male lead, in the musical 'Dear Louise'. She later married Don Ross in 1928.

Gertie continued with her career but whilst performing at the Palace Theatre, Blackpool, she heard that her mother had been admitted to the North Staffordshire Infirmary. Gertie had already lost her father through silicosis. Her mother had remarried to Bob Burden who ran the Swan Inn at Silverdale. Gertie was faced with one of the hardest decisions of her life - whether to return home or to continue with her performance. The old adage 'the show must go on' won the day. Minutes before her appearance, she heard of the death of her mother. Gertie carried on with her songs but the tragedy was a severe blow to her.

Gertie continued with her career until the age of fifty, which was when she had always planned to retire. Ten years later, in 1948, she and Don staged a comeback along with Nellie Wallace and G.H. Elliot. The show, which was called 'Thanks for the Memories' was a great success and ran for three years. Gertie, in that same 'comeback' year was requested to appear in the Royal Command Performance at the Royal Palladium. It was also in that year that she returned to her roots in the Potteries and appeared at the Theatre Royal, Hanley.

Gertie remained a success until she was taken ill with cancer a few years later. She died at her home in London, 'NelDean', on 5th January 1957 at the age of 68. Her career had spanned almost seven decades. She had acquired both fame and respect. It was not surprising, therefore, that to honour this legend of the music hall, the street in Hanley where she had once lived, and where her mother had run a shop, was re-named from Frederic Street to Gitana Street. Gertie was informed of this whilst lying on her death-bed and could only exclaim how wonderful it was.

Gitana Street is near to the street on to which the stage door of the Theatre Royal opened. A fitting tribute to this woman who for so long had been the Queen of the Music Hall.

CHAPTER FIVE

FANNY DEAKIN 1883-1968

Fanny Deakin, born of humble beginnings, became a legend in her lifetime, fighting for the rights of her neighbours and constituents in Newcastle, and for the cause of the good care of Potteries women in pregnancy and childbirth. Nothing was ever too much trouble for this woman, from finding ways to answer practical needs, to working in the arena of politics to bring about legislation that would make a real impact on peoples' daily lives.

Fanny Deakin, known as 'Red Fanny' after her change in politics from Liberalism to Communism, was born on 2nd December 1883, the ninth child of Enoch Davenport, a miner who had come to Silverdale in the 1870s. The Davenport family lived originally in Church Street, then in a shop in Newcastle Street

Spout House Farm where Fanny was born.

and finally at Spout House Farm at the end of Abbey Street.

Fanny had a relatively happy childhood but had already at school begun to show streaks of rebellion. Whilst there she threw an ink well at a teacher, Miss Horsley, for constantly calling her and other children names.

Fanny left school at 13 to help the family with the farm and by 17 she was married. Her 21 year old husband was Noah Deakin, a miner like her father. Fanny and Noah settled in Kinsey Street in Silverdale and began what was reported to be a volatile marriage, sometimes extremely happy, at other times arguing violently.

Fanny had several children, at least six, the exact number is unknown, but all but one died as babies or young children. Only one, her firstborn son Noah, born in 1903, survived into adulthood. From this developed her

A miners' relief station in Newcastle in the 1912 Miners' Strike. These 'soup kitchens' were run by socialist supporters including Fanny. Several mining strikes in the early part of the twentieth century caused great destitution for local mining families, as the miners sort a share of the great wealth the Potteries coal seams had created.

understanding of and compassion for the needs of pregnant women, and her crusade to improve local maternity services.

Fanny began her involvement in politics in 1906 helping Josiah Clement Wedgwood in his campaign to become Liberal MP for Newcastle. She later became involved in mining disputes and strikes over meal breaks. She supported the strikers morally and also practically by running soup kitchens. By 1917 she had fully entered politics having become a member of the Newcastle and Wolstanton Board of Guardians.

After the First World War, along with Colonel Wedgwood, she changed allegiance to the Labour Party and founded a local branch in Silverdale. This proved an active branch and was good experience for Fanny who, in 1921, became Area Secretary of the North Staffordshire Labour Women, followed in 1923 by her election to the Wolstanton Urban District Council. She was the first woman ever to be elected. It was at this time that she became a communist, but such was her popularity the radical change made no difference to her electoral support.

Fanny again became very involved in campaigning for the miners in the General Strike of 1926. She fought against the reduction in wages and the immorality of the injuries and deaths caused by poor mining conditions. She and her son Noah, even produced a newspaper called the 'Wedge' to further and publicise their cause. She was dedicated to the campaign travelling miles on foot every day around North Staffordshire to encourage other mining groups in pit villages. Fanny was, in fact, seen as the leader of the whole mining community, leading processions, fly-posting and constantly championing the cause of these downtrodden men and their families in rallies and speeches.

Fanny's reputation was also growing in the Communist Party itself. She chaired major meetings and also represented the Party as a delegate to Russia. She visited London as a representative of the unemployed. She spoke with Ramsey MacDonald, the Prime Minister, and with her blunt arguments won concessions for the unemployed, particularly for the poor of the area and for pregnant mothers. For them, and for children under five years of age, she gained free milk concessions.

Fanny's political career was hampered, however, by the fact that she was often considered too outspoken. Fellow politicians felt that she was not sensitive enough to the party as a whole and that her individualistic tendencies, whilst successful in militant challenges, were not what the party required, particularly of potential Parliamentary candidates. This is perhaps one of the reasons why Fanny never became an M.P. herself.

Another reason could have been that at this time, her husband Noah was the victim of a terrible pit accident. He was hospitalised for months and on discharge, although he had recovered from his broken ribs and vertebrae, he found he was left with no sense of balance. He was often bedridden and in constant pain. Fanny cared for him and also fought his claim for compensation, which she was successful in. The reduction in their family income meant, however, that they had to leave their home in Kinsey Street and move to a council flat.

Although her political involvement at this time was severely curtailed she still found time to campaign against the 'Means Test'. Demonstrations were held against this test but Fanny was often unable to attend. Some of the demonstrations were violent and this led to many arrests. One young man who was arrested claimed he was not actually at the riots at all - it was a case of mistaken identity. He tried to support his case by claiming that on the day

A J Cook, the National Secretary of the Miners Federation, addressing North Staffordshire miners in the 1926 General Strike. Fanny Deakin marched with Cook at the head of the miners' protest through Newcastle and Wolstanton up to the Marsh.

The Fanny Deakin Maternity Home - a name synonymous with good maternity care in the Potteries from the 1940s to the 1970s. It was opened after many years of campaigning by Fanny.

Fanny Deakin as a
young lady and an
'elder stateswoman'.

6 Kinsey Street was Fanny and Noah's home until 1946 when they had to sell it and
move into a council flat. In 1931 Noah had been badly injured in a roof fall at the
Leycett Pit and would never work again. Surely a modern day saint, Fanny strived all
her life for the good of others while neglecting her own best interests, saving many
lives especially through the free milk she won from Prime Minister Ramsay
MacDonald and through her maternity work.

In 1927 and 1930 Fanny went with trade union delegations to Russia. She is seen here with women miners.

BELOW:
Fanny Deakin was the first woman ever to be elected to the Wolstanton Council. She is on the front row of this photo of the Council taken for the opening of the new gasometer in Chesterton in 1924.

in question, he was actually at the home of Fanny Deakin. Fanny, perhaps somewhat foolishly, backed up his claim, although there were many other witnesses to prove that the man was at the riots.

The result for Fanny was that she was charged with perjury and found guilty at Staffordshire Assizes in July 1932. Fanny received nine months imprisonment and served them at Winson Green Prison in Birmingham. Fanny was purported to be a a model prisoner. On discharge she never really referred to this time again, preferring to put it behind her and to look to the future. Her husband had to be cared for by friends and family through this difficult time.

She had had to forfeit her seat on Newcastle Borough Council when she was imprisoned but on her return she was re-elected with an increased majority. She was also, in 1934, elected to the County Council.

Fanny now followed a more formal and careful route through politics serving as Alderman of the Newcastle Borough Council and Staffordshire County Council. She sat on a wide variety of committees including the Childrens' Committee, the Youth Committee, the Adult Education Committee, the Advisory Committee for Disabled Pensions, the Advisory Committee for the National Health Insurance, the Life Boat Committee and the Local Employment Committee. She was on the Board of Guardians for a total of thirty years.

In 1947 she was responsible for the opening of Newcastle's first maternity home, at a time when specialised maternity provision for working class women was almost non-existent. It was the culmination of her career and the home was always known and respected as 'The Fanny Deakin'.

Fanny continued into her eighties as chairman of the Maternity and Child Welfare Voluntary Committee. She was taken off the Aldermanic Bench in 1949 and in 1951 resigned from the County Council, following the death of her husband. In 1965 she was made an Honorary Alderman of the Newcastle Borough Council in recognition of her years of service to the community.

Fanny died in 1968 at the age of 84. The service was held at Bradwell Crematorium and, in faith with her character, in memory of the Hunger Marches, they played the Harry Lauder song 'Keep right on to the end of the road'. Fanny will not be forgotten quickly. She has left a legacy to the underprivileged of this society through her constant fight for their rights and the betterment of their lives.

Vera Brittain with her son John Williams, and two other famous women authors of her day, her friends Winifred Holtby and Phyllis Bentley.

Vera with George Lansbury at a Peace Meeting in 1938. Vera Brittain, George Lansbury, Donald Soper, Dick Sheppard and Laurence Housman were all prominent international pacifists of the time.

CHAPTER SIX

VERA BRITTAIN

Born 29th December 1893 in Newcastle under Lyme, the great-grand-daughter of Thomas Brittain of Brittain's Paper Mills, Vera Brittain experienced a very loving up-bringing. Her parents were Arthur and Edith Brittain and she had one younger brother, Edward.

Vera and her family moved in 1895 to live at Glen Bank, Macclesfield, so her father could work at the paper mill in Cheddleton. In 1905 they moved again, this time to Buxton where her family mixed in high society. But as a child she visited the paper mills in Cheddleton, and she later recalled happy memories of picnics on the banks of the Churnet or fishing for minnows in a Trentham stream where two aunts ran a school.

Vera was an intelligent person, but from an early age she experienced the inequalities of education offered to women. Vera received her early education from a governess and later went to a boarding school in Surrey. She was not encouraged to develop her education further, unlike her brother. Instead she was expected by her parents to mix in the high society of Buxton and find a husband. But Vera was keen to achieve a good education and in 1914, at the start of the First World War, she persuaded her father to allow her to go to Somerville College at Oxford University.

It was ironically the coinciding of these two things, going to university and the War, that were to alter the course of Vera's life irrevocably. Whilst at university she met and became engaged to Roland Leighton. Roland went to fight in the War and was tragically shot and killed by a German sniper on Christmas morning. By this time Vera had already decided to leave at the end of her first year at university and become a nurse for the period of the War.

She served as a V.A.D. in England, Malta and France. There she experienced at first hand the horrors of war. By the end of the War she had not only lost her fiancé but also her brother and her two best friends. Vera's life was changed for ever. She became a staunch supporter of pacifism, and it was this philosophy, as well as her commitment to equal rights for women, that governed the direction of her life ever after.

At the end of the War Vera returned to Oxford to continue her studies. Here she became involved in supporting the cause of degrees for women. It was not until 1920 that women in Oxford received their degrees alongside men in the Sheldonian Theatre. It was a campaign that Vera was proud to have been a part of.

During the last two years of her time at Oxford, Vera met two people who were to influence her for the rest of her life. One of these was George Catlin, soon to be her future husband, and the other was Winifred Holtby who was to be her close friend until her early death in 1935.

By the time she left Oxford, Vera had decided that the career she wished to pursue was that of a writer. Initially she was better known for her lectures on behalf of the League of Nations Union. She was also co-editor of 'Oxford Poetry'. Within two years of leaving, however, she had written several articles, and two novels 'The Dark Tide' and 'Not Without Honour'.

Vera married George finally in 1925 and had her two children, John in 1927, and Shirley in 1930. Shirley is now known to us better as Shirley Williams, famous SDP politician. Vera's passion for writing did not fade or falter. She continued to produce a massive amount both as a novelist and as a freelance journalist. Two of these included her now famous autobiography, 'Testament of Youth' in 1933 and the novel 'Honourable Estate'.

Vera was also prolifically involved in feminist groups and the Women's Movement. She even began a movement of her own called The Six Point Group. The six goals they followed were:

PENSIONS FOR WIDOWS
EQUAL RIGHTS OF GUARDIANSHIP FOR PARENTS
IMPROVEMENT OF LAWS RELATING TO CHILD ABUSE
IMPROVEMENT OF LAWS RELATING TO UNMARRIED MOTHERS
EQUAL PAY FOR TEACHERS
EQUAL OPPORTUNITIES IN THE CIVIL SERVICE

Vera in her VAD nurse's uniform and her brother Edward in his officer's uniform, visiting their parents in Buxton, 1915.

Above right:
Edward's military grave in Italy 1918.

Vera on the left as a VAD in Malta, 1917.

Vera's life between the two World Wars was filled with her continuous production of novels and articles, and her commitment to womens' issues. However, her personal life experienced more suffering. Her father committed suicide in 1935 and, in the same year, her best friend, Winifred Holtby, with whom she had fought so many political and social battles championing the causes of womens' rights, died prematurely of cancer. Her marriage to George also foundered.

Immediately prior to the Second World War, seeing how international events were developing Vera began to strengthen her commitment to pacifism and in 1937 became a sponsor for the Canon Dick Sheppard's Peace Pledge Union. In 1939 she became involved in the Food Relief Campaign and the India Independence Campaign. For this she was nominated as a British Delegate in the All-India Womens' Conference. Vera's story of her commitment to pacifism can be found in the 'Testament of Experience', another famous autobiography, which she wrote in 1957.

Vera speaking at a peace rally in London before the Second World War.

Following the War, Vera travelled throughout the world to lecture, and she continued to write novels. But her passion for the rights of women and pacifism never failed. By the time of her death, in 1970, Vera had written 29 books, including two volumes of poetry, two autobiographies, other biographies and travel books. She had been involved in numerous pacifist organisations worldwide.

Her greatest contributions were in improving the lives of women and putting the perspective of pacifism into the world of open debate. She was a pacifist but she did not believe in passive acceptance of situations, more the active use of intellect and reason to help civilisation progress. Her example is something to be admired and reflected upon.

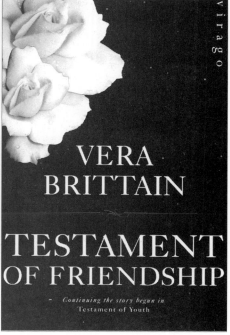

The books that made Vera Brittain famous and which are still popular and freely available in print to this day.

BIZARRE WARE

SMEDLEY SERVICE.

NEWPORT POTTERY
CO., LTD.
Newport Pottery
B U R S L E M
STAFFORDSHIRE, ENGLAND

CHAPTER SEVEN

CLARICE CLIFF

'BIZARRE' - this was the name given to Clarice Cliff's early designs in pottery ware. Bizarre because of the bold, gaudy, geometric 'Jazz Age' patterns she used to demonstrate her unique talent.

The production of this Art Deco ware was the beginning of a short, but highly acclaimed, period of creativity in Clarice's life. Her unique talents have remained for several decades unrecognised, but of late Clarice's work has become highly sought after by Art Deco collectors. Some pieces now reach astronomically high prices. For example, a decorative plate portraying a Mount Etna design recently fetched in excess of £12,000.

This fame, although to a large extent posthumous, is no small achievement for a woman born the middle child of seven brothers and sisters, before the turn of the century, on 20th January 1899. Clarice's parents, Harry Thomas Cliff and Ann Cliff (nee MacHine) then lived in Meir Street, Tunstall. Clarice attended the High Street Elementary and Summerbank Schools in Tunstall until 1912. She left to take up an apprenticeship as an enameller for three years after which she went to work at Hollinshead and Kirkham. Here, Clarice learned the art of lithographing, a technique which a later pottery designer, Susie Cooper, helped pioneer in earthenware. Like Susie Cooper, Clarice attended a local School of Art; Clarice at Tunstall and Susie at Burslem.

After three years of tuition Clarice left art school and obtained a job at A.J.Wilkinsons of Burslem. Here her talents were soon spotted by Jack Walker her decorating manager, and brought to the attention of Colley Shorter, Wilkinson's managing director. The company allowed her to experiment with her own designs, and went on to buy up the neighbouring Newport Pottery Works to act as a base for Clarice's work.

The whole of the pottery industry was at that time experiencing a general slump in export trade largely because of the 50% tariff on exports imposed in the McKinley regime (1897-1901). Despite this, Colley Shorter managed during the First World War to develop new markets in South America and Canada to offset this American loss. Clarice's innovative new designs came at the right time to capitalise on this new trade expansion.

Clarice's designs were not just popular abroad, they became extremely popular in the home markets too. Travelling sales people seemed initially shocked when asked to take out the new ware, convinced that no-one would want to buy it. To their amazement they were returning two or three days later to stock up again! It was following these beginnings that the 'Bizarre' range was launched.

To achieve the effect in 'Bizarre', Clarice experimented with bright colours and designs made up of diamonds, oblongs and squares. Clarice would use imperfect ware to display her talent. It was not long before these 'bizarre' productions became so popular that more staff had to be taken on and trained. These young women later earned themselves the title of the 'Bizarre Girls'. Clarice herself was still only in her late teens when her abilities were recognised.

Clarice went on to have her work shown at many exhibitions. In 1923 her design Tibetan won the Diploma of Honour at Ghent. She also visited Harrods where she would paint her designs on pottery ware in the windows for passers-by to watch.

Not everyone liked her ware, Susie Cooper and Queen Mary, consort of King George V, being two prominent opponents of her designs. Susie Cooper did not admire her work at all, stating quite openly that, *'It was not what I thought of as the epitome of good design'*. Queen Mary was more blunt still, describing Clarice's work as 'awful'. As Howard Watson, collector, has been recorded as saying, *"Clarice Cliff grabs you. It's so extreme there's no shaking it off. It has even destroyed marriages. There are no half measure with Clarice"*. Whether people loved her work or hated it there was no doubt that Clarice had captured the imagination of the Roaring Twenties.

She remained at Wilkinsons where she worked as art director, earning a reputation as a good boss as she continued to oversee the band of workers needed for the constant supply of her work.

Clarice married Colley Shorter, Wilkinson's managing director, in 1940. It is said that Clarice's design work had tailed off considerably by that time. Certainly, the advent of World War Two had an incredibly dire effect on her industry, many of her workers being called up for either the forces or war work. Whether Clarice would have developed other designs will never be known. She retired in 1939 choosing not to go down the road of running her own pottery works, as Susie Cooper had done. Whatever your view of her work, whatever our imaginings about her ability to have produced more designs, there is no doubt that Clarice has left an incredible legacy to the people of the Potteries, her work now being renowned worldwide.

The Bizarre Girls 1931.

Clarice in 1929 and the late 1930s.

'Tennis', 'Tea for Two' about 1930.

Below: Clarice's workshop at Wilkinsons was in the building with the bell tower to the left of bottle ovens.

A painting
demonstration
by the Bizarre
Girls - Clarice
far right.

The Bizarre
Girls

Dame Veronica (C.V.) Wedgwood.

CHAPTER EIGHT

CICELY VERONICA WEDGWOOD

Although born in Northumberland, C.V. Wedgwood saw her roots as Stoke on Trent. She said that *'if anything moves my heart more than a trumpet it ought to be the resounding name of Stoke-on Trent.'*

Veronica Wedgwood, the name she was later known by, was born July 20th 1910, the daughter of Sir Ralph Wedgwood, the sister of Sir John Wedgwood, the niece of Josiah Clement Wedgwood, the Stoke MP, and the great-great-great-granddaughter of the famous Josiah. Although he lived 150 years before her, she said *'she still felt the lively presence'* of this great ancestor upon her family especially when she visited the family home or the Wedgwood Works at Etruria. It was here that she watched potters skilfully throwing work and learned a great lesson in life, that *'a great part of the secret of achievment is perseverance and hard work'*.

The extensive Wedgwood family believed in constantly improving themselves, working for their education and livelihood with this 'labour and perseverance', and Veronica demonstrated this throughout her prolific career as an historian and authoress. She entertained ideas at a very young age of becoming a second Shakespeare, beginning her first book of essays 'The Velvet Studies' at the age of twelve. Her father thought that the work would never end and in an effort to stop her filling more and more notepads he advised her to consider writing history - *'even a bad writer may be a useful historian'*.

Veronica received an exclusive private education under a Swiss governess, during which she gained her life long love of the Continent and foreign languages. She went on to the Sorbonne in Paris and then to Margaret Hall at Oxford where she gained a 'first' in History at the age of 21.

But she did not sit back and rely on her family. When her father died she took a job as a publisher's reader and set out to pursue her career in writing. She worked for the weekly art review 'Time and Tide' for many years. Her first book was a biography of the 17th century politician Strafford and it was typical of C.V. Wedgwood's thoroughness, and her desire for accuracy and fairness in history, that she would, at the very end of her career, rewrite and re-evaluate this work when the politician's original papers became available for the first time.

Her first book was followed by a lifetime's work in historical biography, specialising in European and British history of the reformation and counter-reformation period. Her books were important academically but were also very popular and were printed and reprinted in many hundreds of thousands around the world. Her books include: The Thirty Years' War; The King's War; The King's Peace; Oliver Cromwell; Montrose; William the Silent; Truth and Opinion; Richelieu and the French Monarchy.

In an evaluation of C.V. Wedgwood, Elizabeth Johnson praises her ability to make history readable. She had acquired the skill of popularizing history without making it sensational and was still regarded as ' a historian of true distinction' by her contemporaries. She retained a sense of the individual person in history and how they were affected by the circumstances and events of their day. C.V. Wedgwood said herself, *'The human personality....cannot be left out of the record or treated as a mere ornamentation in the story of mankind.......you cannot judge a man until you know what he was. Personality is not a surface thing; it is the very core of character.'* By combining her love of history and literature, she was able to produce such flamboyant, yet accurate, historical books.

During her lifetime Veronica received many honours including many from universities around the World. She was made Dame Veronica Wedgwood in 1968 and awarded the Order of Merit in 1969. She served on the Arts Council, on Royal Commissions, and as a trustee of both the Victoria and Albert Museum and the National Gallery. She was also President of the English Association. She gave many lecturers - and it was one measure of her generosity to others that she often gave lectures without charge.

She died in 1997 aged 87. She lived for nearly 70 years of her life with her close friend Jacqueline Hope-Wallace

CHAPTER NINE

SUSIE COOPER

Susie Vera Cooper was one of this century's most renowned and talented pottery designers. Not only did she design, she developed completely new techniques, ran her own businesses and succeeded on a national and international scale. Susie Cooper was a pioneer in her field and certainly deserves recognition in this hall of fame.

Susie came from a family which had no interest or talent in the arts or design. Her family ran a farm in Tunstall which she helped to run when she left school, Mollart House, at the age of 15. Her father had died when she was eight and now her mother was going blind. These difficulties did not stop her finding the time to go to night school. Susie attended the Burslem School of Art and learned about wood carving and dress design as well as pottery. She had initially wished to pursue a career in dress design but changed to pottery and applied for a scholarship to study this further.

Susie was successful in this and in 1921 enrolled full-time at the Burslem School of Art to study pottery design and decoration. She went on to study the interior design of theatres in London when she was still only twenty years old.

On her return from London, in 1922, she joined the Hanley based A.E. Gray and Co. She gained there an invaluable grounding and experience. It was here she learned the techniques and problems of producing earthenware. Susie began to design her own pieces of ware at Grays and was the first woman potter to be allowed to sign her own pieces. Such was the popularity and

The young Susie.

The Burslem School of Art where Susie trained.

The famous Leaping Deer used in many Susie Cooper designs of the 1930s.

standard of her work, in 1924 she became Gray's resident designer.

During the same year she presented her own work alongside Gray's at the British Exhibition in London. Susie went on from this success to become responsible for all displays of Gray's ware and in 1925 represented them at the Paris Exposition.

In 1926 Susie achieved worldwide acclaim with the production of her now famous " Deer Vase". Susie's work was both innovative, and stylish in sharp contrast to Clarice Cliff's bold, geometric designs. Susie Cooper had abandoned these designs to pursue the development of a more distinctive ware that she felt was more pleasing to the eye. She did not admire Cliff's work saying it was *'not good design'*.

It was hardly surprising that Susie began to run her own pottery firm in 1929, and she produced much impressive work. Susie was always considered a good business woman, a kind person who felt a strong sense of moral obligation to her work force. For instance, in the 1930s she was reputed to have

The Leaping Deer used as a statuette

deliberately turned to designs she knew would sell, to ensure her staff had work and wages. She is credited with the distinction of bringing the pottery industry out of the recession during that difficult time.

In 1932 her work was noticed by the entrepreneur John Lewis at the British Industrial Fair. He ordered the 'Polka Dot' series for his chain of stores and so began a good business relationship with Lewis and a resultant expansion for the works. By 1933 Susie was producing fifty different decorations for tableware and was using her pioneering technique for washbanding on many of them. She received major orders from many dignitaries including the Royal Family. Her Kestrel dish was chosen to be shown at the British Art in Industry Exhibition in 1935. This again led to increased demand for her work including orders for her earthenware in all of Peter Jones' restaurants.

During this time Susie also pioneered the lithograph which she used on her now famous 'Dresden' ware, ordered by Edward the Eighth in 1936.

Susie's innovative skills did not stop here. This talented woman went on to pioneer inglaze decoration. She was labelled a 'workaholic' by many people but she put her prolific production down to pure enthusiasm for the job. Susie's great achievements were finally recognised formally in 1940 by the Royal Society of Arts when she was named Royal Designer for Industry. She was the first woman to receive this honour.

Susie's tidal wave of success was marred in 1942 by the burning down of her factory, the Crown Works at Burslem. She made the decision to remain closed for the remainder of the War period but quickly re-opened in 1945, setting up production herself. By 1950 she had bought another pottery firm, Jason China in Longton. Susie continued to develop new styles and patterns including the radical cone shape and the Black Fruit design. Her success was again marred in 1957 when the Crown Works again burned down.

Not daunted, Susie set herself new goals in life, in particularly moving into the field of china production as well as earthenware. She wanted to make china accessible to all people while ensuring it was china of style and quality. This was a goal she achieved time and time again.

The sixties held their own problems for her, however, and Susie Cooper Ltd was absorbed into the Wedgwood Group. Susie continued to ceaselessly produce innovative ware for them including Corn Poppy and Glen Mist. In 1980, when the

Susie at the height of her career.

Crown Works closed down for the final time, John Ryan, Managing Director of William Adams and Sons (also part of the Wedgwood Group) moved Susie to their factory premises in Furlong Road. Here she produced such well-known designs such as Meadowlands and Inspiration which became High Street names for stores such as Tesco and Boots. Susie really had made good china and earthenware accessible to all!

Susie was recognised locally for her vast achievements by the award of an honorary doctorate by Staffordshire University and, in 1993, with an honorary degree by Keele University. She had already achieved national acclaim through the award of an OBE in 1979.

Susie finally retired at the age of 84. She had, until then, lived at the Old Parsonage in Dilhorne but then moved to enjoy her retirement in the Isle of Man. Susie did not stop working however. She experimented with painting and moved onto other projects including the restoration of the square where she lived with the aim of it achieving 'listed' status.

Susie was still working up until her death in 1995 at the age of 92. She was given a memorial service at St. Peter's in Stoke led by the chaplain of Staffordshire University, Reverend Graham MacNamee.

Susie's career was long and prolific. She made an incredible impact on the world of pottery production and design. Her early works particularly are now collectors' items and classics in their own right. Her importance in the field of pottery can not be overestimated.

Susie put her success down to *'independence'*, *'trusting her own judgements and intuition',* and mostly *'by being her own boss.'* This coupled with her hard work, love for the job and sheer talent could not fail to make her one of the world's finest potters. She is, indeed a Potter to be proud of.

The 'Cube' shape pottery of the early 1930s.

Susie was born in Stansfields, Burslem. Her parents later moved to Milton and this picture of a Cooper family group was taken at the Coopers' Farm in Milton in 1913 when Susie was 11. Susie is 4th from the left on the front row just behind her mother.

Bold designs for A.E.Gray.

Dresden - a beautiful pottery print from the 1930s.

1950s Susie Cooper.

The Crown Works in the 1950s.

Crown Works after the fire in 1957.

Classical tube-
lining decoration
on a tile by
Charlotte Rhead.

Below:
Burgess and
Leigh plaque.

CHAPTER TEN

CHARLOTTE RHEAD

Charlotte Rhead came from a long line of prominent artists and pottery designers. Her paternal grandfather, George Rhead, was an art master and he started the School of Art at Fenton. He had three sons, Frederick, Charlotte's father, George Wooliscroft Rhead, who was Superintendent of Art Instruction over a group of London schools, and Louis, a famous poster artist in America. Charlotte's father, Frederick, was a famous pottery designer, a lecturer and an author. Her mother, Adolphine, was the daughter of C.F. Hurton, a important flower painter. Charlotte's two brothers, Frederick Hurton Rhead and Harry Walsham Rhead, were well-known in the American pottery industry in East Liverpool, Ohio.

Charlotte learned much from her talented family but she developed into a very important pottery artist and originator in her own right. She specialised

in 'tube lining', a old process where pottery is decorated with liquid forced through a narrow glass tube, which she perfected and took to a new level. The pattern produced is in relief - with raised lines on the pottery. She produced many subtle and fascinating designs with the technique, which she had mastered in early teens at Wood and Sons, and later, when she worked for Burgess and Leigh, she trained others to use this very difficult skill.

Charlotte first worked at Wood and Sons of

Charlotte in her Burgess and Leigh days.

Burslem, where she experimented with tube lining on tiles. She later moved with her father, to Crown Pottery in Burslem. She also worked for a while at Ellgreave Pottery in Burslem. Here she produced her famous red-bodied tableware with highly individual designs which are backstamped 'Lottie Rhead Ware, Ellgreave' - 'Lottie' was the Rhead family's pet name for Charlotte.

She now moved to Burgess and Leigh where she stayed for five years. The work she produced here is very collectable and is backstamped 'L. Rhead', but her most prestigious work was Crown Ducal Ware which was produced when she went to A.G. Richardsons. Most of this work is backstamped 'C. Rhead' and the designs include Golden Leaves, Byzantine, Foxglove and Wisteria.

Her final place of employment was with H.J. Wood where she worked as the Art Director until she died in 1947. Many feel that Charlotte Rhead is vastly underrated as a pottery designer and would rate her as equal in ability to Susie Cooper and Clarice Cliff. Some even say that her skills surpassed theirs. Whatever, Charlotte certainly has a place amongst the most famous of potters from Stoke on Trent.

A.G.Richardson's Gordon Pottery in Tunstall in the 1930s.

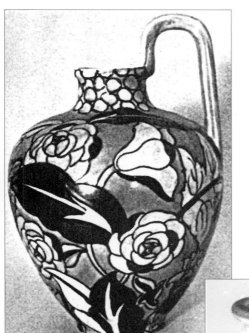

A Wood and Sons
'Bursley' jug by
Charlotte Rhead.

A Crown Ducal vase of
about 1937.

Girl who beat The Beatles

Jackie Trent with husband Tony Hatch celebrating their Number One in the charts in 1965.

CHAPTER ELEVEN

JACKIE TRENT

Jackie, born Yvonne Burgess on 6th September 1940, was the daughter of a coal miner, and she always had music on her mind. She sang with the Bignall End Babes at the age of eight and was 'discovered' at the age of eleven by Carroll Levis from Canada. In 1956 Jackie was chosen as the North Staffs Coal Queen. By sixteen she had auditioned with the BBC and made a recording with Ted Heath and his Orchestra. She later went overseas to entertain British and American troops.

By the time she met Tony Hatch she was a performer in her own right and had already written many of her own songs and music. It was this music which had impressed Tony when he first auditioned her for a recording contract in 1963. Jackie Tremaine, as she was initially called, became Jackie Trent - thus maintaining links with her home town.

Jackie and Tony began writing songs together and in May 1965 the ballad 'Where are you now' reached number one in the charts replacing the Beatles' 'Ticket to Ride'. Jackie and Tony married in August 1967 and became known as 'Mr and Mrs Music'. On the day of their marriage their record company released 5,000 copies of their record 'The Two of Us'.

The duo went on to write now famous songs such as 'Don't Sleep in the Subway Darling', 'Call Me' and 'I Couldn't Live Without Your Love'. Their singing clientele included Petula Clark, Scott Walker, Val Doonican and the Sandpipers. Jackie and Tony are also famous for the theme music to 'Mr and Mrs' and the now world famous 'Neighbours' theme.

Jackie and Tony went to live in Australia, mainly for tax purposes, and remained there for many years. Jackie has recently returned to live in Kent following the break-up of her twenty eight year marriage. Jackie is touring for the first time in many years in a successful revival of the Cole Porter musical 'High Society'.

Jackie lives with her mother in Sevenoaks. Her daughter, Michelle, has recently married. She is an actress and has appeared opposite Dennis Waterman in 'On The Up'. Jackie has a son, Darren, who is also in the music business.

Anthea over ten years.

CHAPTER TWELVE

ANTHEA TURNER - LUCKY LADY?

Well, is she just a lucky lady or does she have brains and talent to go with those good looks that have many times brought her the callous criticism of being a 'blonde bimbo'? Well, having met her I am of the opinion that she is both intelligent and beautiful! She has, undoubtedly been in the right place at the right time and had good management and guidance from her then husband/manager Peter Powell, but it was Anthea who at the end of the day had to go into the interview for the job, and persuade them that she was the right person for the TV presenter post being advertised.

Anthea's determination to achieve and do well in all that she does is so apparent in the way she talks. She is quite inspiring. She believes that if someone wants to achieve something then they should not allow things to come in the way of that achievement. People should set goals and aim for them with true determination. *"If a woman really wants to do something she will find a way. If she doesn't then she really didn't want to do it at all!"* she says.

Anthea knows that she has been blessed with both good looks and opportunities in life, but what she has made of those things has been her own doing. The criticisms of being called a 'bimbo' and a 'ruthless women' have hurt her but she has learnt to deal with them. She knows quite well that they would never perceive a man who was highly focussed and successful in such terms.

Anthea's career has gone from strength to strength. Her stint in 'Blue Peter' was followed by two and a half years on the GMTV 'Good Morning Sofa' and 18 months as the golden girl of the nations' first Lottery Show. Anthea has proved her versatility and professionalism over and over again. Latterly she has completed several one off shows such as the 'All You Need is Love' show and a Christmas special with the Royal Navy. These have been followed by the successful series 'Pet Power', 'Turner Around the World' and currently the prestigious travel series 'Wish You Were Here'. Anthea has also been recalled to launch the new look Lottery Show.

She and her sister, Wendy Turner, have also written a book called "Underneath the Underground", stories about a family of mice who live in the Underground in London and have a series of adventures in places such as Harrods, Wimbledon and the Houses of Parliament. Anthea and Wendy plan to do a follow up series to this successful childrens' storybook.

All this is not bad for a girl who hails from Norton, the eldest daughter of Jean and Brian Turner. Brian runs a family business, Turnercraft, and Jean is a trained teacher. Jean gave up her career to care for her middle daughter Ruth, now deceased, who was born with spina bifida. Anthea pays credit to both parents who sacrificed so much for them all. The thing she appreciates most of all is the time they invested in all of their daughters. Her parents are, she says, the nicest people she knows.

It was also her parents' care and concern for her that helped her cope with the difficulties of dyslexia and bullying at school. A move to St.Dominics' School for Girls, where Anthea received proper help for the now well acknowledged condition of dyslexia, proved to be a turning point in her life where she was able to grow in confidence and begin to develop her aspirations for a stage career.

Anthea's first break came when she graduated from the AA breakdown information service to doing the traffic reports for local BBC radio. From there she moved to Signal Radio as the record librarian and later worked in the PR Department. She dated Bruno Brooks for a long time and moved with him to London when his own career as a Radio One disc jockey took off. Anthea then began her own career for Sky TV as a video jock, quickly moving to BBC1 with her big break on Blue Peter.

The rest is history. Her rise to fame has been phenomenal but well earned. Anthea approaches everything with enthusiasm and does not believe in the stand back approach. She knows that her current jobs generally open more doors than they shut. Anthea's future is therefore sure to be star studded.

Anthea's private life has recently hit the headlines showing that even the most glamourous and successful amongst us are not exempt from the pains of life. In my interview with her Anthea made no secret of the fact that she would like to have started a family but this dream and hope will now perhaps have to wait a little longer for fulfilment. Anthea knows that when that time comes, the privilege of her position means that she will probably be able to both be a mum and continue her TV career.

But, until that time, Anthea is continuing in a truly professional style to be the star that she has become. I believe that she has the ability to do what ever she puts her mind to. I feel certain that she will succeed for a long time to come.

Interesting facts:

Birthday: May 25th 1960.

Favourite Stories as a child: Enid Blyton's Secret 7 and the Famous Five.

Favourite TV Shows as a child: Folly Foot, Blue Peter and Banana Splits.

In 1996 Anthea was voted:
> The celebrity single men would most like to jet off with on holiday.
> Having the sexiest voice in the country.
> Show business personality of the year.

Favourite games as a child: Garden wigwam, Batman, police with walkie talkies.

Main Hobbies: Horse riding, swimming, gardening and shopping!

Women in Show business she admires most:
> Judy Finnegan, Cilla Black and Esther Rantzen.

Father, Brian Turner.

Anthea with
Bruno Brooks.

Anthea with
husband Peter
Powell.

The Turner sisters are very close.

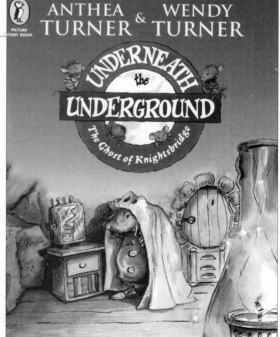

Wendy with Mum, Jean.

CHAPTER THIRTEEN

WENDY TURNER

Wendy, sister of Anthea, was born on 5th June 1963. The family's second daughter, Ruth had been born on exactly the same day four years' earlier. Ruth died at the age of fifteen having suffered with spina bifida from birth. Wendy and Anthea both realised that Ruth took a good deal of looking after but their parents, Jean and Brian, were careful to ensure that both of Ruth's sisters received as much attention as possible. Both were encouraged to develop to their greatest ability and both, amazingly, followed the same careers, at slightly different times.

Wendy trained in dance, speech and drama and starred in professional plays with the Shelton Repertory Theatre and also with the North Staffs Operatic Society. She has worked in the media in a variety of capacities including video production and freelance journalism for magazines such as OK and Honda Car Magazine. In November 1995 Wendy and her boyfriend Ceri Glen test drove a Honda Civic to Lapland. Whilst there they visited Father Christmas with letters from Children all over North Staffordshire.

Wendy's real break in came when she was chosen for the part of Cinderella in the Theatre Royal's 1995 Pantomime. This was a part her sister had also played in 1991 in Winchester. Following her success in this Wendy was approached to be a guest on 'LIVE TV' after which she was asked if she would be interested in presenting. Wendy has since presented 'Absolutely Animals' for Channel Four and has already been signed up for another series. She also presents the successful series 'Pet Rescue'. Her work with these programmes has taken her all around the world.

Wendy has also already taken two forays into the world of publishing, first with the childrens' book 'Underneath the Underground', which she co-authored with her sister Anthea, and second with her own book 'The Absolutely Animal-Free Cookbook' which gives her own vegan recipes.

Interesting facts:

Wendy is a committed vegan.
She is a great lover of animals: Amongst her pets are two ponies, a dog, two cats and two mice.
Wendy earned her first professional wages dancing as a Diddyman in Burslem!
Favourite book: 'Rebecca' by Daphne Du Maurier.

HER MAJESTY'S

❖ A STOLL MOSS THEATRE ❖

Chairman: JANET HOLMES à COURT
Deputy Chairman and Chief Executive: RICHARD JOHNSTON
Managing Director: ROGER FILER
Manager: MARK HAYWARD

CAMERON MACKINTOSH and
THE REALLY USEFUL THEATRE COMPANY LTD
present

The
PHANTOM
of the
OPERA

Starring
DAVE WILLETTS

JILL WASHINGTON   MARIO S. FRANGOULIS.
AND
MICHAEL BAUER   ETHAN FREEMAN
JULIA GOSS   RAMON REMEDIOS   SALLY SMITH

at certain performances
IRÉN BARTÓK
plays the role of 'Christine'

Music by ANDREW LLOYD WEBBER
Lyrics by CHARLES HART

Additional lyrics by RICHARD STILGOE
Book by RICHARD STILGOE & ANDREW LLOYD WEBBER

Based on the novel 'Le Fantôme de l'Opéra' by GASTON LEROUX

Production design by MARIA BJÖRNSON   Lighting by ANDREW BRIDGE
Sound by MARTIN LEVAN
Production Musical Supervision ANTHONY INGLIS
Orchestrations by DAVID CULLEN & ANDREW LLOYD WEBBER
Musical Staging & Choreography by GILLIAN LYNNE
Musical Direction by MARTIN YATES

Directed by HAROLD PRINCE

World Premiere performance at this Theatre Thursday October 9th 1986

CHAPTER FOURTEEN

THE SINGING SISTERS

The Washington sisters are but two of North Staffordshire's many celebrated and talented opera singers. The Singing Sisters, Lorna and Jill Washington, were born on 20.1.53 and 4.9.55 respectively, daughters of Roy and Minnie Washington. The family originally lived in Burslem but have subsequently moved to Biddulph in the Staffordshire Moorlands where Roy and Minnie still live.

Roy himself comes from a family of tenors and he and Minnie were delighted when both children at an early age displayed an interest in singing. It was Minnie who first noticed Lorna humming songs she had heard on radio even before she could talk! Minnie distinctly remembers her as a three year old, trooping through the neighbourhood with a line of children behind her, all singing 'The Teddy Bears Picnic'! Another favourite was the 'Happy Wanderer' which she had heard on the radio and immediately began to hum. When Jill was about two years old she also began to entertain, starting with 'Kiss me, Honey, Honey, Kiss Me.'

When the two sisters were about 11 and 13 the family went on holiday to Llandudno. Whilst there they entered the talent contests which were held at the Bandstand on the sea front. Lorna insisted on entering the adult section. Despite her young age she still won second prize with her rendition of 'The Hills are Alive with the Sound of Music'. Jill sang 'O Shepherd Boy' unaccompanied in the childrens' section and won first prize. This was a good start for the two girls who would later take up singing as a career.

Roy and Minnie continued to encourage their daughters in their musical talent throughout their school careers. Lorna began with piano lessons which she quickly taught to her sister on returning home. Jill, as a result began to attend lessons herself. From there Jill progressed to the flute and Lorna to the violin. Following this, both began to have singing lessons.

During their years at Thistley Hough School for Girls their talent was developed under the tuition of Miss Brown, music teacher and particularly by Miss Wardill, the Head of Music. The school had a great commitment to the pursuit of excellence in musical performance and sought to constantly encourage the two sisters in their talent.

The two girls sang in school productions and, through the school, gave presentations all over North Staffordshire quickening their interest in operetta and extending their repertoire. A highlight of their time at Thistley Hough was singing in the Englebert Humperdink Opera 'Hansel and Gretel'; Lorna took the part of Hansel and Jill the part of Gretel. The opera was performed in its entirety. For girls of 16 and 13 respectively this was in fact a great feat of stamina and the performance was received as a resounding success by school and family audiences alike.

In 1970 the school turned comprehensive with no sixth form causing Lorna to move to St. Dominics to complete her second year in the sixth form. Even so the two girls continued their singing lessons together with Miss Wardill and that year performed in Purcell's opera 'Dido and Aeneas'. Lorna took the lead part and Jill the role of Belinda.

On completion of 'A' Levels both were accepted into the Royal Academy of Music. Lorna won an Associated Board Scholarship. Both, although at different times, completed the performers' course and both studied under Marjorie Thomas. The young women enjoyed successful student careers. Lorna sang a wide range of parts including Offenbach's 'La Jolie Perfume', the lead part in Puccini's 'Sister Angelica' and Snegourochka in Rimsky Korsakov's 'Snow Maiden'. Jill played Nanetta in Verdi's 'Falstaff' and Titania in Britten's 'Midsummer Night's Dream'. Whilst she was appearing as Titania, Jill was 'talent spotted' by scouts for the D'Oyley Carte Opera Company.

Jill went on to sing as the principal soprano in the 'Mikado' and the 'Pirates of Penzance' and later sang in 'Ruddigore.' She stayed with them, save one year returning to study further at the National Opera Studio. Following this she joined the Glyndebourne Opera Chorus where she understudied. She later sang at both the Dublin Grand Opera and the London University Opera in the part of Grettel in 'Hansel and Gretel'. She also took the role of Angele Didier in 'The Count of Luxembourg' and Peep-Bo in the 'Mikado' for Sadler's Wells New Opera. For Opera 80 she took the role of Micaela in 'Carmen' and Blonde in 'Il Seraglio'. On the lighter side she sang in the Welsh National Opera tour 'Novello - a chance to dream' and played Tuptim in 'The King and I'. She has also been a TV and radio celebrity in Thames TV 'Top Cs and Tiaras' and Radio Two's 'Friday Night is Music Night'. On one occasion the two sisters starred together!

All these experiences proved a good training ground for Jill, and whilst singing in the chorus of 'Phantom of the Opera' she was asked to audition for a lead role. She initially declined the offer but was later recalled by Lloyd Webber to audition for the part of the understudy to the lead role. Christine. Clare Moore had moved on to another company and the number two, Jan Hartley-Harris, took her place leaving the number two understudy part vacant. Andrew Lloyd Webber was thrilled with Jill's superb singing talents and she was given the part. The family as a whole were ecstatic at her achievement and watched Jill perform many times. They are proud to be able to tell people who ask 'who is singing Christine tonight' that it is Jill Washington, and the reason they know is because she is their daughter!

Jill sang the part of Christine for two years, then had a break to tour in the operas 'Giovanni' and 'Marriage of Figaro'. She returned to the 'Phantom of the Opera' in London for a further two years, and following a period in 'Don Giovanni' in London, she is again back as Christine.

She now lives in London with her husband, Timothy Evan-Jones, whom she met whilst studying at the Royal Academy. Timothy is himself a renowned Welsh Tenor. In her leisure time Jill enjoys fishing and golf as pastimes. She still pursues avidly her career in music with the help of her London agent. She has returned to Stoke-on-Trent several times over the last few years to appear in different performances. She recently appeared at the Victoria Hall to sing in the performance of 'HMS Pinafore' which was narrated by Richard Baker OBE. It was so fitting to see this native of North Staffordshire return to her home ground to share and display once again her impressive musical talent.

Lorna has had no less prolific, prestigious and varied a career since the training pathways of the two sisters parted. Lorna has, since she left the Royal Academy, sang all over the world in her equally beautiful soprano voice. She has sung several times in Dubai and also before the Sultan of Oman. She has sung in East Germany, before the Wall came down, in Japan, Kenya, Portugal, Cyprus and Switzerland. A much travelled opera star!

She has also appeared on radio in 'Friday Night is Music Night', where the two sisters sang duets together not only heard by the nations millions but also watched by almost the entire family in the studio. Other achievements include Verdi's 'Requiem' in the Albert Hall, Violetta in 'La Traviata' for Gemini Opera, Barbarina in 'The Marriage of Figaro' and the role of The Girl in 'Emperor of Atlantis'. This was for Mechlenburgh Opera's highly acclaimed production in the International Opera Festival.

Lorna is currently busy in Opera Cabaret which she hopes to bring to the North of England with her own company. This would provide the public with the opportunity of hearing opera and music of the highest quality at private banquets and functions. Lorna also spends time training stars of stage and screen to sing.

She currently lives in London with her husband, Roy McIntosh, a computer expert and the only one of the group not to have a career in music. Roy and Minnie are no less proud of him than the rest of the singing family. Roy and Minnie know that their daughters have succeeded in life. Opera, they say is a competitive business with often little advice on careers after the academic training. However, with a combination of their natural born talent, encouragement and a lot of hard work, Jill and Lorna deserve their reputations as the sensational singing sisters.

Jill Washington   Lorna Washington

CHAPTER FIFTEEN

BRENDA PROCTOR, BRIDGETT BELL, GINA EARL AND ROSE HUNT

The 'Nice Girls' are reputed to want to write their own story in their own way. This short resumé will, I hope, serve to give them the honour surely due to a group of women who are legends in their own time, and will not, in any way detract from their own perceptions and views.

The 'Nice Girls' shot to fame and nationwide renown in the Spring of 1993. The four women, the wives of miners, occupied the Number Two Pit at Trentham Colliery in protest at the Government's closure policy of mines all over the country. For these four women, their families and their communities this was more than a fight for jobs, it was a fight for their future, their heritage and their lives.

The four women's lives are bound together with a long history of mining families. Brenda's father was a miner who lived at Meir and she married a North Staffs miner. Rose's father, who originated from Amritsat in India, worked as a miner in the Scottish coalfield near Bannockburn and later at Hem Heath. Rose herself married a Scottish miner. Bridget's father was a miner from Geordieland. Gina's father had been a miner in the Welsh coalfields.

The women were also united in their struggle against injustice to miners in the past, present and future. The women formed a singing group during the 1984/5 Miners' Strike to encourage people on the picket lines and to spread the truth about not only their own plight but the plight of all working class people trying to hang onto an honest job.

The women continued to sing together over the succeeding years at socials, rallies and many picket lines. The women form part of both the North Staffs Miners' Wives' Action Group as well as the Justice For Mineworkers Campaign for whom they still continue to work on behalf of the 996 miners and their families who were sacked but the Coal Board during the 1984/85 strike.

It was as part of the NSMWAG that their famous dash for freedom and justice was born. Their tale begins in Sheffield in January 1993 when the National Women Against Pit Closures Group decided that direct action was

Brenda and Rose with Arthur Scargill of the National Union of Mineworkers.

● The pit protesters receive their cheque from MPs George Stevenson and Joan Walley, MEP Mike Tappin, and county council leader Bill Austin.
Photo: DAVE TRUMBLE

Nice Girls off to Paris as part of cultural exchange

needed against the pit closures proposed by the Government. In October 1992 the Government had announced the closure of 31 pits giving 30,000 miners one week's notice. The miners and their families took the Coal Board to the High Court whose decision was that the proposals were in fact illegal.

The miners and their families knew, however, that this was not the end of the story. It was with the certain knowledge that the fight would continue and, with the encouragement of their recent legal victory, that pit camps were set up outside ten of the most threatened pits. The North Staffs Miners' Wives' Group took their protest to the gates of Trentham Colliery setting up a 24 hour camp. It was from this concerted effort to register their opposition to the closures that the 'Occupation of the Pit Head' came about.

The three originators of the plot were Rose, Brenda and Bridget all of whom had seen picket action before outside pits and at the Wapping Newspapers in London. Gina, the fourth member, was not recruited until the last minute. The need for secrecy was paramount. The three had already gained the support of a 'mole' who had worked down the pit and was prepared to help them with information about the security and layout at Trentham.

A trip to 'Wilkinsons' followed, for the purchase of essential goods and the tools for 'entering the premises'. It was with some amusement that they met later - finding Gina dressed in purple silk they assumed she was going for a weekend to Brighton! They could not have been further from the truth. At 3.20am on Wednesday morning 12th May 1993, Brenda, Bridget and Gina occupied the Number Two Pit Head. Their original intention had been to take-over the Tower which would have had facilities for cooking and keeping warm. This attempt was thwarted by the security firms forcing them to run frantically anywhere until Gina found an open door, and led the others into the pitshaft tower.

They remained there for three days and four nights whilst Rose, on the outside, co-ordinated press releases and as much support as she could muster. The group were supported by women from Liverpool, MPs, Councillors, the Bishop of Stafford, and hundreds of miners and their families.

Courage must have often failed the four both inside the pit and outside in the camp, but their determination to fight on for what was right kept them going. They knew that, in some strange way, whatever the outcome they would never really have lost. People would always know that they had struck a blow for the right for miners to work and to keep their families and communities together.

On Saturday morning of the same week the three women were brought out by Arthur Scargill. He made an emotional appeal and speech applauding their actions and their bravery. They left the pit singing their defiance and their right to fight for what they believed in. The women had made living history. This living history that has been immortalised since by Peter Cheesman's production of 'Nice Girls', a musical documentary of the women's occupation of the mine. The play has run successfully time and time again at the Victoria Theatre and, in May 1995 was taken to Paris to resounding success.

The Nice Girls continue with their fight for the rights of the working class person. They continue to sing their songs of history and freedom. They continue to strive for a better future for all working people.

Photograph John Harris

The Nice Girls

CHAPTER SIXTEEN

ANGELA SMITH

Three times World Squash Champion, Angela Smith, began her famous career by training as a physical education teacher. She soon realised, however, that this was not what she wanted to do with her life. Having developed an interest in squash she now pursued it with enthusiasm and with a view to it becoming her life's interest.

Angela originally played squash in the amateur circle. Her big break came when she was picked to go on tour to Australia with the England team. Then, having gained vital experience in these tournaments, Angela became the first woman to turn professional. She lived then in an environment where men laughed at her, saying that women could not make a profession out of it. She felt many times that men came to watch her for the novelty value, just to ogle her body and to taunt.

Angela, however, defied this chauvinistic attitude with her strength of character and sheer skill at the game of squash, gradually gaining the respect of everyone. In her playing career she won more than 100 international caps for England and Great Britain and was in the top three women players in the World for a period of seven years. In 1989 she won 35 titles including the hat-trick of the British Open, the British Closed and the World Championship. As a professional and exhibition squash player, and then later as a coach, Angela has carved out an enormously successful career for herself. In 1979 she was the official coach to the United States Men's Squash Team!

Angela Smith
Womens' Squash World Champion and
World No 1 1989.

Stoke on Trent College Sports Centre.

Angela receives one of her many national trophies from Gordon Banks, the
famous England footballer.

Angela went on to manage the prestigious, state-of-the-art fitness centre at Stoke-on-Trent College, and take a Masters Degree in Sport. She now works in Birmingham for "Pro-Golf".

Angela's love of sport has taken her all over the world. She lived in New York for three years (where amongst others she coached Jackie Kennedy), the Bahamas for seven and Barcelona for four, all in connection with her career. And to think, until she first left home, Angela, who was born and brought up in Bucknall, thought that Stoke-on-Trent was the centre of the Universe!

Angela succeeded not just because she had the opportunities but also because she had the determination to do so. This determination again brought her success only last year, when she competed alongside champions such as Steffi Graff and Martina Navratilova for the title of the World's Ultra-Fit Woman in Florida. Angela is modest about her victory saying she thought her age would go against her. It was her drive to do well, and to raise money for charity, that kept her going. Angela is often involved with fund raising but keeps a low-profile on this.

Angela now lives happily with her husband in Stoke-on-Trent. She is keen to encourage other women to do well and to achieve in whatever is their chosen work. She admires the determination of successful women such as Anita Broderick and Martina Navratilova, who have each experienced male opposition, and not only survived but gone on to achieve greatness due to their strength of character and ability.

Angela also pays tribute to her parents who encouraged her to choose and pursue her own career. Angela says they have always been a support to her and she feels she inherited some of her determination from them, especially her mum.

Angela would like to see Stoke-on-Trent become a centre of excellence for women in encouragement to achieve, not only in the world of sport but in all fields. She believes the new City Council could be national forerunners in this drive by promoting more awareness days for women, more well-women clinics and a forum where successful women could speak to other women about their success.

Angela is an asset to this City both in what she has contributed to its culture but also in her forward thinking concerning women. Angela's success, and the drive behind it, is an inspiration for those equally determined.

Above:
Three young ladies of the cast of the Potteries Theatre Company practising for the musical Pinocchio. The company has been established for 8 years.

Kate Bailey national junior fell-running champion.

CHAPTER SEVENTEEN

OTHER LOCAL ACHIEVERS AND STARS OF THE FUTURE

In this chapter I have tried to highlight other women who have made their mark locally and also some of the up and coming stars. Of course there will be many I have missed but what I really want to do is show the exciting prospects for women in so many directions and careers now. Are you amongst the stars of the future? Who knows - all that extra effort put in now might pay off in the future.

DANCE

Roxanne Weaver of Trentham achieved fame when she was chosen to dance in 'Scenes from Alice in Wonderland' with Wayne Sleep and the National Youth Ballet. Roxanne has been dancing since she was three and wants to become a professional ballet dancer when she is old enough. She is supported in her ambition by her parents who take her to day classes with the prestigious Central Ballet School in London each weekend. Roxanne, a pupil at Trentham High School, has already appeared in the West End and seems to have a successful career ahead of her.

Another promising ballet dancer is Laura-Beth Bailey from Birches Head. She also has been performing since the age of 3 and, like Roxanne, appeared in 'Scenes from Alice in Wonderland' with Wayne Sleep. Laura-Beth played the part of the shrunken Alice. She won a scholarship to train with the British Ballet Organisation in London. She does other forms of dancing including jazz, tap and modern. Her family, and the Angela Beardmore School of Dancing where she began her dancing career, are very proud of her. Laura wishes to become a dance teacher.

Roxanne and Laura-Beth appeared together on Blue Peter to dance excerpts from the Ballet of 'Alice in Wonderland'. They performed the Rose Garden scene and 'The Mad Hatter's tea party'.

Louise Butler of Brown Edge, also of the Angela Beardmore School of Dancing won a national scholarship with the British Ballet Organisation. Louise has the potential to acieve great things in the future. Rachel Rimmer of Stockton Brook and Lindsey Wright of Knypersley, also achieved the same scholarship to dance with the Northern Ballet School in Manchester.

Rachel Brown of Clayton has already played at the Bloomsbury Theatre in London in their production of the 'Nutcracker' Suite. Rachel played the part of a snowflake. Rachel, who trained at the Minnie Skerrett School of Dance in Newcastle, has also been a junior member of the Royal Ballet in Birmingham.

Claire Lapthorn of May Bank has well and truly honoured the support she received from local organisations by finishing her three year course at the North Ballet School in Manchester. She won the place against great competition. Her mother is immensely proud of her.

Zena Cooke of Clayton comes from a dancing family. She has starred in Aladdin at the Theatre Royal and also won a place with the national Youth Ballet. Zena performed in a gala evening at the Sadler's Wells Theatre in London.

Rebecca Boulton of Milton succeeded in winning a place at the Northern Ballet School of Manchester despite an accident as a toddler which injured her feet. Rebecca trained for five years with the British Ballet Organisation in London.

Sadie Wright of Longton and Emily Bunce of Eccleshall, both formerly students at the Mary Humphreys School of Dance, won places at famous dance schools. Sadie studied at the London Studio Centre in London on a performing arts course and Emily at the Rambert School of Dance in Middlesex. Sadie has previously appeared in 'Revuetime 88' at the Theatre Royal and 'Joseph and his Amazing Technicolour Dreamcoat' and 'Alice in Wonderland', both with the London Lewis Ballet.

Marianne Smith of Basford was nominated by the British Ballet Organisation for a scholarship to the Moscow Dance Academy. She trained at the London English National Ballet School and sacrificed many things to achieve her dream. She has had to leave family and friends but is driven on by her ambition to be the best.

ENTERTAINMENT

Cheryl Richardson of Handley Street in Packmoor produced a variety show including disco dances, tap, ballet and a magician. Over 18 youngsters took part in the show 'The Next Generation' which raised money for Childline and the Rwanda Appeal. Cheryl has won a two week summer school place at the Sylvie Young Theatre School in London and her ambition is to produce and direct.

Gabriella Panichi of Hartshill won a £2,000 grant to further her career at the Mountain View Theatre School in London. Gabriella won her grant from an Oscar winning actor who wished to remain anonymous.

Rachel, Becci and Rebecca Morrel of Hillwood Road, Madeley, were first discovered on the Barrimore Show on television. They formed a cabaret group called 'Indians' and performed in cabaret in Blackpool. They also played opposite each other in the play 'Bugsy Mallone', Rachel playing the part of Blousey, while Rebecca took the role of Tallulah.

Deborah Gibson, stage name April Martins, appeared in the Oscar winning film Evita, in the part of Peron's early girlfriend. Deborah, from Dawlish Drive, Bentilee, and a former pupil of Willfield High School, now lives in Slough and continues to pursue her acting career.

Vicki Gotham of Queensbury Road, Normacot, won a place at the 'Fame' school founded by Sir Paul McCartney. She was one of only 15 students accepted out of 5,000 hopefuls, and she is currently studying for a degree in acting at the Liverpool Institute. She did most of her training at the Amanda Andrews Drama Studio in Blythe Bridge.

Sarra Brian of Werrington currently appears on TV in 'Living Room Legends', a daily show showing people's home video entertainment skills. Sarra changed careers from a budding lawyer to TV presenter. She thoroughly enjoys her job and believes she won the post because of her wit and personality which she attributes to being a child of the Potteries!

Kerry Wilson, of Trentham, is well known on the cabaret circuit as an enormously talented comedienne. Her big break came on the Jonathon Ross 'Big, Big, Talent Show'. She had given up a holiday to appear on the show and was both surprised and thrilled when she looked into the audience, to see her family sitting there, cheering her on. The TV company had flown them all over from their holiday to see Kerry's TV debut.

Sian Foulkes of Gower Street in Newcastle wants to be a film director. She won first prize locally and third prize nationally with her 3 minute film 'As I See It' where she portrayed the world around her. Sian suffers from dyslexia like Anthea Turner, but this has not stopped her achieving.

Kerry Dean played four performances of the lead role in Cinderella in 1997. She is a professional dancer and wants to pursue a career as an actress.

Suzy Turner of Tunstall took the two year national Diploma for Performing Arts at Newcastle College. She is currently appearing in '100 Years of the Silver Screen' in London, dancing to themes from films through the ages.

Emma Stirland formerly of Edward Orme High School and Newcastle College is playing the understudy for the female lead in 'Dial M for Murder' at the Apollo Theatre, Shaftesbury. Emma has already played the debut part of Sheila Vendice. Emma comes from Ashley near Newcastle.

PAINTING, PHOTOGRAPHY AND MEDIA

Sophy Barrow of St. Wulstan's Primary School won 1st prize for 7-11 year olds in a national photo-journalism contest. She won £500 for herself, a camera and films and £500 for her school. Sophy's article covered the effects of litter, open-casting, road and light pollution on the environment.

Katie Bird won 1st prize in a national competition with the Prudential. She painted a boy who was imagining his future as either an astronaut, a saviour of the planet or a cook. She won £250 for her school, who bought her a watercolour set as a reward.

Gemma Bradley entered the Britain in Bloom painting competition. Her painting of 'April' was chosen as the best out of 1000 submissions.

SCIENCE

Sumanjit Sethi won the 'Europe's Young Scientist of the Year' award in 1997. Sumanjit submitted research she had done into asthma at the North Staff Hospital Medical Research Unit. Sumanjit is the daughter of Dr. Kulwant Sethi and Manjit Sethi.

SPORT

In October 1997 Emma Brammer, 13, and Dawn North, 25, were set to make history as England's first women amateur boxers. Dawn and Emma registered with the Amateur Boxing Association when the rules were changed governing women's access to the ring.

Dawn, from Penkhull, and Emma, from Stanfields, were trained for their historic bouts by coach Pete Stoneway at the George Amateur Boxing Club in Burslem. They had to wait for their first fight though, because their entrance into the male dominated world of boxing caused a furore amongst those who found it hard to accept female participants in a violent sport.

The bulk of the criticism centred around the belief that women are at greater risk of harm in such a physical sport. The argument of free choice versus safety raged for many weeks. For Dawn and Emma, however, their choice was simple. Men see boxing as a sport. So do they. They enjoyed it in training and looked forward with eagerness to their first fights, which finally occurred once the initial opposition had died down.

Dawn eventually became the first English woman to fight in an ABA bout. Her fight was against Mandy Griffiths of North Wales at the Whitland Dairy Sports and Social Club in South Wales. Dawn fought a three round match and won on points, 10 - 8. Dawn was injured in the match and sported a large black eye for some time but she is determined to carry on in the sport, and to aim even as high as the ABA championship itself.

Emma, aged 13, also continued bravely on despite the opposition and some outright bullying, and went on to win her first bout against Andrea Prime from Leicester. Emma was the first schoolgirl to fight in the amateur boxing world.

Whatever peoples' views, Emma and Dawn have shown true grit and determination to succeed in their chosen sport.

Another female achiever of the 'ring' is Klondyke Kate, real name Jayne Porter. Jayne has experienced a long and successful career in wrestling. For over two decades she has been a popular attraction to wrestling fans, and was the first woman to fight at the Royal Albert Hall in 1987. She has fought many times at the Victoria Hall, a central venue for wrestling for 50 years.

Jayne, once known as 'hell in boots', finally hung up those boots in

1996. She has since studied for GCSEs and computer skills and hopes to get a job working with underprivileged children. She is also involved in the Willfield Community Education Centre, where she helped to run a youth club and set up a social group for women on Bentilee with her friend Vicky Wilkinson. The group, 'Big and Bold' is for larger women. Jayne, herself over 20 stone, wanted to encourage those women who did not want to become smaller, but rather wanted to grow in confidence.

Jenny Booth and Janice Burton are disabled swimmers. Jenny, from Cross Heath in Newcastle, made world history in the Atlanta Paralympics as part of a team that broke the world record in the 4 x 50 metre freestyle relay. She also came back with a bronze medal for the 4 x 50 metre medley relay.

Janice Burton has competed at four Paralympics. She won 3 gold and 4 silver medals at the Barcelona Paralympics alone, and before she embarked on the Atlanta Games she had 20 medals and 42 international awards. In 1995 she swam in the European Disabled Swimming Championships in Perpignan, and won three gold, two silver and one bronze medal at this event. In 1996 she received a special citation from Staffordshire Moorlands Council in recognition of her achievement at the Atlanta Paralympics where she achieved a silver and two bronze medals.

Nikki Daniels from Tunstall won the English Schools Championship for middle distance running at the Don Valley Stadium in Sheffield. She also took the 800m in 2 minutes 15.59 seconds at the AAAs Tournament. Nikki's sister, Kerry, is also a champion runner having represented England at cross-country.

The list of Emma Ward's running achievements is already quite long despite being only 15. In 1995 she ran in the under-15 girl's age group and was top of both the 800 and 1500 metre rankings. She was chosen to represent England in the TSB's Schools' International at the NEC, where she took the gold medal in the 1500 metres intermediate event.

MARTIAL ARTS

In 1995 Stella Dawson won the World Championship in Kung Fu. Stella is not only a black belt in Kung Fu but also in kick boxing. Stella comes from Etruria and works as a figure painter. Stella has ambitions to teach martial arts. She trained at the Lau School of Kung Fu in Stoke. In May 1996 Stella won the Senior Individual Award at the City's Sports Awards.

Sarah Whalley won silver in the Martial Arts World Championships in Prague at the age of 12 in 1996. Sarah of Hanley and Holden Lane High school trains at the Hanley Martial Arts Centre

Amy Cooke and Rachel Whitehurst became British Judo Champions at the age of 13. Both girls are part of the Biddulph Judo Club.

In 1996 Lucy Beech of Newcastle won the junior title of the Central Region Karate Championships in Stourbridge.

Kim Heath of Lightwood won the European Women's Kata Championships. Kim, who works at Spode, won her title in Paris. She now plans to aim for the world title in her chosen sport since the age of six.

BADMINTON

Sammi Tudor and Louise Williamson became County Badminton Champions in October 1996. They also received a nomination for the inter-counties championship as a result. Sammi, from Cheadle, won the Player of the Year in 1995. She played for the England under 13 team in the Home Countries Tournament in Bradford. She helped them achieve second place.

GOLF

Lisa Hackney of Trentham is one of Europe's top women golfers. Lisa started at Trentham Golf Club at the age of 12, and turned professional in 1991. She has played throughout the world particularly in America where recently she received the Rolex Rookie of the Year Award.

Lisa won the Welsh Open title in 1996 and was fifth in both the US and British Open Championships, but the height of Lisa's career so far was when she was selected to play in the Solheim Cup, the women's equivalent of the Ryder Cup. Lisa is now ranked 13 in the LPGA world rankings.

HORSE RIDING

DAWN HUNTER of Biddulph Moor became national champion in carriage driving at Royal Windsor in 1995. She also won the Tebay Driving Trials, and at Barnard Castle. She now competes against international drivers.

Francesca Smith won the All-British Supreme Mini Championships at the age of 5. Her sister, Phillipa, had won the same title three years previously. Phillipa and Francesca have been riding since they were just four months old. Between them they have won dozens of trophies. Francesca will compete this year in the Royal International Horse Show.

Camilla Fox has been stunt riding since at least 9. She was taught Roman stunt-standing by her father Gerard Naprous of the Devil's Horsemen stunt riders. Camilla, who hails from Leek has appeared on TV in 'True Tilda' and her riding stunts were covered by Blue Peter. She looks set to follow in her father's footsteps - he has appeared in Euro 96, Braveheart and Black Beauty.

In 1996 Corinne Collins was selected to represent Great Britain in international show jumping. She was one of only five people chosen to represent Britain at the competition in Germany.

SWIMMING

Heidi Earp of Trentham has been winning major swimming competitions since 1993. Her ambition to swim in the next Olympics in Sydney is a great possibility. Heidi, who swims with Newcastle Amateur Swimming Club, has been the National Age-Group Champion, the Inter-County National Swimming Champion and a finalist in the European Junior Championships.

SLALOM CANOEING

In 1996 Laura Blakeman was selected to represent Great Britain in three World Cup races. She is the youngest person ever to be selected for Great Britain's Slalom Canoe Team. Laura narrowly missed being selected for the Olympic Games in Georgia in the same year but hopes to make it next time in Sydney. Laura lives in Seabridge, Newcastle, and has been trained by Andy Neave of Stone and Penny Briscoe in Nottingham.

MODELLING

Kerry Forster of Biddulph Moor achieved her ambition of becoming a model after signing up at a model agency in Hanley run by Samantha Edge. Kerry was just 13 at the time. She has appeared on Channel 4's Big Breakfast as well as modelling for fashion shows, sportswear and bridal shows.

Stephanie Stokoe became the 'Face of 1997' last year. She won an all expenses trip to London for a photo shoot. Stephanie was, unknown to herself, entered for the competition by her aunt. Although not keen at first Stephanie is now pleased her aunt took the step. Stephanie was a student at Fenton Sixth Form College at the time studying for 'A' Levels in Law, Sociology and Business Studies - brains as well as beauty!

WRITING

Leek born Pam Hurst wrote her first novel in 1995. Her book, 'Angel of the Moorlands', was first devised by Pam as she cared for he mother during a long illness. Over the years she developed it and refined it until she felt satisfied that it was complete. The book covers the life of Jennie, orphaned at 10 in the mid-1800s. Her life is turbulent but in her heart she has one lifetime love - and you'll have to read the book to find out who that is and what happens!

Pam is thrilled to be recognised as a novelist. She is already a keen amateur dramatist. Pam continues to write and we will look forward to the development of her literary career with interest.

The art of writing romance is Dilys Gater's great achievement. Dilys, of Clayton, has written over 30 romances during her lifetime including her latest novel 'Celtic Wise Woman'. Dilys says of all the things in the world that will die one day, romance is not one of them!

Joan-Ann Grindley of Meir has written two books on the subject of tales told in pubs! A Pint Sized History of Stoke-on-Trent and A Pint Sized History of the Staffordshire Moorlands depict the lives of people who frequent the pubs and the history of the area. Joan-Ann has been told some tall stories in her time and never ceases to be amazed at the things she finds out. The mother of four children, she is still busy finding stories for more books.

Priscilla Masters has achieved her dream of becoming a nationally acclaimed authoress. Priscilla of Knypersley has written a series of crime stories starring Inspector Joanna Piercy. 'Winding Up the Serpent', 'Catch the Fallen Sparrow' and 'A Wreath For My Sister' are all published by Macmillan.

Newcastle born Mary Selby had her first novel published in 1996. 'A Wing and a Prayer' was particularly successful in Canada, and 10,000 copies were sold in England in the first few weeks after it was published. Mary, who now lives in Suffolk, continues her career as a novelist.

MUSIC

Denise Leigh from Hartshill went through to the Midlands finals of the National Festival in Warwick in 1996 following an outstanding performance at the Biddulph Music Festival in 1995. Denise, who is partially-sighted, would like to be a full time performer or possible teach music.

Karen Stephenson of Madeley and in her twenties has had a most prestigious career as a celloist. She studied at the Royal Northern College of Music in Manchester, went on to a scholarship with David Strange at the Royal Academy of Music in London, and became the principal celloist with the European Community Orchestra. Karen has performed throughout Europe with the London Symphony Orchestra and the Welsh National Opera Orchestra. Latterly she has played with the BBC Philharmonic.

By the time Davinia Caddy of Alsager had reached the age of sixteen she had become the youngest person to achieve the Performer's Diploma of the Guildhall School of Music. Davinia's chosen instrument is the flute. She won a place at Chethams' School of Music in Manchester where she hopes to continue her career as a most talented musician.

BIBLIOGRAPHY AND SOURCES

Vera Brittain: A Life	Berry and Bostridge	Chatto/Pimlico
Testament of a Generation	Berry and Bishop	Virago
Susie Cooper: An Elegant Affair	Bryn Youds	Thames & Hudson
Clarice Cliff: The Bizarre Affair	Griffin and Meisel	Thames & Hudson
Clarice Cliff Collectors Club		
Art Deco Knits	Melinda Cass	Blandford
The Sentinel	Stoke on Trent	
Leek Post and Times	Leek	
The Way We Were	John Abberley	The Sentinel
Victorian Women's Fiction - Marriage, Freedom and the Individual	Shirley Foster	Croom Helm
Mrs Craik, A 19th Century Novelist - A Study of Victorian Attitudes	Ann Thistleton	
Vera Brittain: Feminist in a New Age	Muriel Mellown	
Gertie Gitana: Queen of the Halls	John Godwin	The Bugle
Victorian Palace of Varieties: The Story of the Music Hall		
Silverdale People	Joyce Holliday and Gerald D'Arcy	Staffordshire Libraries
People of the Potteries	Editor Dennis Stuart	University of Keele

I wish to thank the Staffordshire County Council Library Service, and particularly the Newcastle Library, for permission to use photographs from their publications.